In The VentingII

s.v.h

In The VentingII

ISBN: 978-1-7350198-0-2

I really want to thank God first for creating me into an amazing man that I am today. Without God I am honestly nothing. Next in line are all my loved ones who I hold close dear to my heart. Those who helped me create such an amazing art piece in my life to bless others as you have blessed me. Lastly, I want to thank all of you who are taking the time out of your day to read this book. Along with the past book, and many others ahead of this one. Thank you for existing. Your existence matters.

Art can be expressed in many ways

This is just my way of expressing it

VII

July 2018

here I am

I am here

I’m becoming a man people

want to hear

through the setbacks

and set ups

the fall backs and mess ups

I am here

I am alive and well

I am here

The other side

recently relationships haven't been my thing
don't get me wrong I love to sing
singing in places like a shower or car
even up underneath a star
I look up into the night sky and see you
my shining star
I just wish you weren't so far

Rapids and bridges

we would always go by the river

and watch it flow down the stream

from the hot day all the way down the cool sunset

the river itself was flowing slow and steady

while the skies turn into a mixture of cream

afterwards me and her along with a few of our friends
would hang by the campfire

this was a summer memory of me when I was
younger

when things seemed a little easier back then

Wonder

epic like nebula

stronger than mixture that formed the formula

never trip

let's take a trip to this space

off to this place where the cool wonders of space

we win the race from the exhaustion

every time we hear the clock of the tick of the tock

but quick now

we don't have much time

travel with me back in this time and come back to me

it's time

now it's my time

I'll take my time with you

take a shot

now take a shot for me

I was messed up

this is messed up I know

at least we know

what poetry can do for us

June's Spring

every new beginning comes from an ending
after it all ends there will be a new beginning
like baseball idea of having the game nine innings
flowering making this vernal
in our time of seedtime
the fresh scent of fertile
the sun will hit just right as we love to do for one
the smell of the vanilla coming from the flowers
reminds me of the candle scents from the candle store
I love the spring

A work of art

I look at the things God created in this life
how the skies became blue
to our vision as the day of time sits in
even though the ground has its ups and downs it's
still able to perform art
from the hills and mountains
the animals that walk on such amazing wide fields
found themselves into art
but when I see the women God created
I see every single woman that walks on this earth
the creation and the defiance of a woman is amazing
ladies love yourself for who you are
with every curve that you were blessed with
every piece that is known to be treasure that is placed

on you for your eyes to see

and every movement you take

always remember you are art

Contract (A deal is a deal)

I don't mind telling you the truth

I don't mind hurting your feelings

so do me and you a favor

tell me the truth

even if it hurts me

In

inside

deep down inside

I’m there

I’ll always be there

Ardor

show me the real you

whenever you have the chance to

show me the truth

give me soul

August 2018

if it is so

say so

if not so

say it ain't so

The art of blur

humans lie

why

because speaking the truth isn’t enough

Start

I have plans for you
I have plans for us
I’ve been thinking about you
on a balcony watching the city view
we can start with foreplay
the taste of your lips and rubbing your chest
switching it up
kissing on your spots in that way
it’s your body but you’re going to do as I say
don’t say
just do
and I’ll reward you
with these times two
we are having fun

your body is meant for me

as you are for me

that’s why I know what to do with it

I’ll please it

no one will see it

I’ll treat you

like royalty

Trophy

you’re my novelty

make your way to me

come to me

Waves

deep within the ocean
with the waves we share
we give each other motion
you give me life
yet you cut me deep
these tides aren't always
going to be so peaceful
they will be ugly but
I promise it will be beautiful
currently I'm current
like the ocean when the wind relaxes it
when it comes to you and I am observant
measuring all your beauty
all your shine with your glow

you are the motherly heaven

you are my obsession

you are my blessing

Cumulous

as we lay here looking up at the marshmallows

you asked me what I see

I responded to you a pillow and blanket

a big stack of puff laying in a basket

within the moment of mist

we kissed

Tender Dove

hello first love

we met so many times I feel like

but it never stopped me to love

my first time running into

you I was a youth

watching my mother and father love

showing me the truth

I grew up and experienced

a love that was new to me

at the time

one that I cherished

but I messed that up

few more years into the future

and I was still stuck

I grew up cherishing

giving and receiving feelings of yearning

the enchantment of sex and the flame of desire

just wish I knew what love was for me

September 2018

there she was again

and here I go again

watching her and observing her

writing and wishing

that I gained the courage to go talk to her

she was taking me back

schooling me back into grade school

wishing I had the courage

to get up and talk to her

never mind

maybe one day we will talk again

maybe one day we will dance again

The change within the season

leap out into the open
leave yourself with the wind and
let yourself be gone with the it

You and me

red dress that symbolizes her taste of strawberries
without stress that her ex used to cause to her
she glances at me
writing a love letter
but this isn't about her
this is about me
the revealing of the flower
letting her hair down
and loving her endlessly
loving her intimacy

Acoustic

I love the way you make my heart feel
it feels so real
almost too good to be true
I've woken out of my sleep some time ago but even
when I was sleeping you appeared to me the same
as you appear now
you smiled and kissed me
how do you do it
give off the same energy as the sun and the same
feeling of the water that surrounds me of the tide
which comes from the crystal cool waters of the
ocean and now
I'm lost at sea

Red

I caught myself licking and biting my lip thinking
about you

To whom

I got problems

you got problems

the solution equals us

Nothing more Nothing less

I hurt myself when I expect from you

hurt myself when I expect less from you

I just hope nothing but the best for you

Reborn

I got over that hurt

I got over that pain

things don't seem the same

things don't feel the same

I'm not the same

I'm more sane

I've found peace

I've found beauty and soul

most importantly I found myself

Waving skies

cold puffy rain drops
they fall below the zero skies
they fall on our surfaces

Free dream

she lays like a rose petal

the beauty of sex appeal

she lays there still

showing her color

she lays there

and there I am

looking

seeking

visualizing

on what we will engage ourselves in next

The side of the other

thanks to you

I’ve become part of you

now I will never know how

it feels to be me again

loss rounds

eventually I will give myself to you

I'm just not ready to

I'm not scared of opening to you

starting over again isn't something I'm not so quick

to rush myself into again

Open risk

I'm going to give into you and your ways

I just hope you're ready for my troubles

Goodnight lullaby

give all your troubles and worries to God
then allow the stars in the night sky along
with the moon to help you sleep

Half crescent

I’ve been catching myself looking up at the stars
and lately
majority of the lately it’s been up at the moon
I don’t know if it’s because you’re on the other side
sitting on top of it or hiding behind it
or perhaps it’s because you’re looking at the moon
like me I would get into a habit of letting the cool
skies kick in and knock me out on the rooftop
no matter the occasion just know I can feel you
I just hope you can feel me too
I’m sure I’ll see you soon

Milk

and just like that the moonlight became her spotlight

The moon

you do remind me so much of the moon

you showed me your beauty and I started to go crazy

Solstice

you’re golden

just like your energy

it’s hard to replace it

because I never want to

Energy

share it with me

show me

and I will show you what it can do

when two people are creating and building

share it with me

bring it to me

bring me your energy

"Good morning."

She said to me with her light voice that matched perfectly with her smile.

"Good morning" I replied to her. "I see that you've slept well." She rolls her eyes as her smile enlarges.

She turns over and picks up her phone that was lying next to her on the counter.

"Ugh I'm going to be late. I wasn't even supposed to be here all night. It's going to be your fault if I get into trouble today with my job." She says as she puts on her clothes.

"The lies. You and I both know this won't be the last. Therefore, it isn't not my fault."

"Hmm. Well I guess you're right about that." She walks on the side of my bed and kisses me.

I enjoy the moment as she starts walking toward the door and I follow her.

I kissed her once more before I let her go. I open the door and waved at her from a distance as

she begins to disappear into the distance.

Lost Count

you can have it all

truth be told there isn't a truth

we became so lost in the truth

we believed it could set us free

you were lost

but I found you

we are brand new

oh how I want to die

let's fly

let's fly away

I just want to die

let's fly away and fly away

oh how I just want to die inside your love

you came in and left whenever I decided to do right

Silk

she dances to the song

singing in perfect tune

this is what happens when you

make a beautiful happy

Little, Little

she hears her favorite song

as she dances to her favorite song

she starts to feel the love that surrounds her

the love that she had within from the beginning

just took the right tune and possible melody

Into the intro

a beautiful day

I can see her everyday

each day

day by day

Peaceful spirit

the air she was giving me

was received

did her a favor in return and gave her new meaning

of life as she did for me

Sooner than later

the flowers in the garden will grow soon

you too shall grow

together we will grow with one another

Zacchaeus

in the tree is where I’ll be

in the tree is where you will find me

in this tree I am free

Her favorite song

good morning early birds

you are here for a reason

whatever the reason

make it last each season

Problem #908

it's crazy how
people find a way
to fight someone and tease
them with their problems
but can't seem to manage problems
of their own

The journey

I know they say silence is golden
but is it really when you hold in
the problems you face by yourself
is it golden when you've seen not few
but many of the wrongs of the world

I'm not here

you don't love me

you only love the idea of me

the happiness that I give to you

is abused and misused

you can't love me

for I am neither you nor me

Lost

numb to the pain

love that is lost and now driven insane

lost in the mood

For you

I need you to care as I care for you

pray for me as I pray for you

protect me

strengthen me

love me most importantly

don't ever leave me

especially when you need me

Dreams and ponder

good morning my love

I fantasize about

the day our lips touching again

to give you a feeling of love and protection

every time you're around me

soon the day will come my love

soon

In between the lines

you are blinded by the things you can see

that's why you can't see

me

Truth

you want the truth but

but somehow you keep coming

up with the lies you tell

that are true

truth is it's you

Emotional flame

love

even if the world forgets how to love you

love

even if he can't hear you or see you

love, you

Coffee

I saw you yesterday and knew you were my today

telling you this everyday

Twinkle star

all the stars are outside but here on the inside
I've got my own
waking up late at night wondering
if this is all a dream
I turn to the side and there you were still
sleeping so peacefully
so quietly
I kissed your head and held you close to me
never wanting to let my star go

Yur-self

run as fast as you can

the truth is going to find you

faster than the lies of what you stand

Superstar

as you wish upon a star

they wonder what life would be like

to become super nova

Inspire the fire

love is such a beautiful thing

let’s keep the desire to inspire on fire

Cherry blossom

there she was again
except now she was standing in front of me
at some distance away
nothing but the cherry blossoms on the path
they lay
a sudden cool breeze that sends a message
to my body raising the hairs on my arms
not from the wind that swifts
not from the flowers in the sky
but from the feeling she sends to me
she sends to me a melody of feeling
a feeling of healing

Unforgettable

I remember you introduced me
to the taste of your lips
it was just as I wanted it
just as I needed it to be and thought it would be

Outlook

rest yourself

ease your mind

and free yourself

I miss you

I feel a little silly
thinking about the many
days of memories in the past
if only we had more
time to make those days last
now you’re some time away
so many miles away
now those miles are turning into days
and those days are turning into weeks
you’re fading away
fuck I miss you

I've missed you

now we have arrived

you came

we laughed and smiled

kissing away the pain

and then we came

fuck I've missed you

One and two

hello I’m lonely

so lonely that no one hurts me

I’ve become so lonely that no one abuses me

tired of living fake happiness

and living a life of things that use to be

I’m here now

using this loneliness as my happiness

no matter how you chose to read this

this loneliness is my happiness

Process

thank you for waking me up this morning

It’s because of you I have awaken

If we didn’t know then we know now

now we are feeling

the healing

Untamed

I was never you

it's because of you

I refused to be you

I'm not the animal

but I am the beast

Twisted Addiction

are you happy

do you feel happy

here

you are happy

you do feel happy

Path of Pathway

after all

the water streams

like a waterfall

you'll stand tall

Four Sixty-Seven

we didn't have much time left

with only

no that's not it

there was a time back when I was four

and saw six and met seven

no that isn't either

here is the truth

time is valuable and shouldn't be taken for granted

on this day September 17

I have four sixty-seven in my account

no not four hundred and sixty-seven

but four dollars and

sixty-seven cents

I promised myself same time next year when the
book is published this part of the book
will be read by many around the world
and I will speak on it

Shadow

hate to tell you this but they will start to think you're

crazy

they will have no idea what you are talking about

I hope you're ready

Who

it's not safe here
it isn't safe anywhere really
they're out there
watching me
watching you
while I am talking to you
they are listening
shh they're listening
the calls we make are never safe
if I can be honest with you
we don't even need to make a call
I always find it odd but
more so familiarly strange

when I am walking alone in a crowd
I find myself making eye contact with someone
even with the "friendly" grins that stretch itself
from cheek to cheek gives me chills

Their dreams, Your nightmares

trust me

I know what it's like

to be in that dark place

that makes you feel like you are alone

I know what it feels like

to be the only one that knows what's going on

to know that there is so much more

than what they may make things appear to seem

I know the feeling

I've been there

I'm here

What if this is what it is

what if all of this is a "just"

just so you can get adjusted

13

there's someone in the room
I can't see who it is because it is so dark
but I know someone is there
touching me
not physically but
I can whatever it is looking at me
I have no idea what to do
the worst thing about it is
that it is aware of that
that's why its standing there
possibly to taunt me
there's this strange breeze that surrounds the whole
room causing things to feel still and blue

I lay there in my bed tying to sleep it out

trying my best to ignore it

having the covers to only protect me

that's when I hear the voice whisper speak out

to me

thirteen

Inferno

I've watched you within the years do your work
I had to sit and be quiet while you
lie, cheat, steal, and kill
the relationship I tried my best to keep alive
well no more
no more shall I or anyone else go through this hurt
and pain you put me through
even though I may be burning on the inside
you're burning on the outside now
and as the flame starts to rise
I'm watching the smoke float in the sky
along with all our memories of both good and bad
good-bye halo
hello inferno

Absolute worst (A very short story)

The storm was getting worse by minute and it felt as though we were in the middle of nowhere. Underneath the night sky. Everyone around me was getting scared and quite frankly I was getting scared too. The winds were blowing hard enough to the point I could hear the train. Even though I saw people screaming I couldn't hear them. Not even the woman in the dress. Am I going to die here?

In some way, I flashback to earlier in the day where there was a sun in the sky with the blue skies and no clouds. How beautiful the girl that was walking had on this beautiful green dress that would move by the sway of her hips. Now that same girl is here crying and screaming out for help.

A glass window brakes from the windows and the shatters reached across our faces. We all started to hurdle next to one another hoping and praying we will make it out of this disaster. I've had many bad days in the past but at that moment I felt that it was my absolute worst day.

Lost in space

it must be nice to
I try to
but I fail to
it used to be because I would
feel as though I am forgetting something
which would cause me to jump
out of my sleep and wake up panting
now it's because my sleep almost
feels like its repeating itself
except it's a different day
a different outfit to switch
from day to day
leaving the house to go somewhere
I know I may not be happy being there

but I keep going there

as though I will find my answers there

when the answers are simple

wake up please

Drainage

you give

then you take

what you give

you just take

what is it you wish for

because I wish that this love didn't exist

The great indoors

my growth grows it’s best when I am growing inside of you

What do you want?

don’t do it because you love me

do it because you want to be happy

do it because you want to be free

Direct Message

I think about the day I will finally meet you
when I am finally with you
constantly at random times
within my days I think about you
spending most of my times thinking of you
thinking about me being with you
and then it hit me
I am with you
miles away you can feel me
and I can feel you without us touching each other
I am there with you as you are reading this
you hear a voice
my voice
you hear me

and you feel me

you feel all of me inside of you

just as I feel you wrap around me

were locked in

I feel your spirit

even though I am not there I am filling your spirit

no matter what mood you are in

I am always bringing you to this mood

I don't know you

nor do I know who you are

but with this feeling I will make use to

Imperfection (uniqueness)

it's in our nature to be imperfect
finding out the true beauty and the art in things is
what makes things perfect

you are what you are

consume your water

consume your nutrients

consume the sun my little sunflower

and watch yourself grow within the sun

Fate or fortune

we both went after each other

with no expectation

we went after each other

with no hesitation

I’ve always been told

it isn’t good to gamble

yet here I am

here we are

October 2018

we were here

we were all here

ylenol syad

it’s just one of those days

we will have our lonely days

we will have those days

the lonely days

Colder weather

I'm sick of the lies

and I'm tired of the truth

nothing you say or do works

maybe it's not you

maybe it really is me

up(side down)set

maybe one day I won't write about you

with the way you treated me

how you misunderstood me

confused me

abused me

how you used me

maybe one day I won't write about you

maybe I'll write about someone new

Moonlight shadows

silence falls

in the shadows of the hallways

the light shines and so do I

Home

there is no home

but at least we have the astrodome

November 2018

I don’t want to overdo it

because then you’ll be telling me

that I’m over doing it

I’m not use to it

this is something I am not use to

It sucks because I can’t force it and have it my way

just got to take it day by day

Right place, right time

I was digging you
you were digging me too
we had our shares of wrongs
so let's make things right
I don't want to be right all the time
I want to feel what's right
what is best for me
and what is best for you
we can't rush it
it's our time
we are here now
in our time zone

Real spill

I'm going to make this last long as I can

before you leave me

then ill end up back where I was before we met

cold with a heart

most of all lonely

YOUr happiness

so you die

not knowing who or what

when or where

or knowing why

and maybe even not knowing how

but at least you died happy

not trying to know everything about anything

but you died happy living your life loving yourself

and knowing yourself well enough to create a certain

type of knowing to yourself

Someone like you

wish there were more like you
someone like you

Mirror

flawless. pure. absolute

-perfection

6,000 questions

is this who you want

is this what you want

is this when you want it

is this where you want it

why do you want that

how so

questions I often ask myself frequently throughout the day that leads into a place I won't go

Red synonyms

it wasn't about me

it was more so about her

it's always been about her

but she sees me

so

she chooses me to be the chosen one

to give and release all of her

fantasies and desires out in the open

she trusts me

not because she hears me whisper in her ear to do so

but she feels as though

I can make her daydreams come true

I whisper and she moans

she moans to the sound of my voice

that fits now so perfectly with her fantasy

after I moan in her ear

she moans again to me

finding her hands on me

trying to reach out to me

not only because she can't contain herself

but she doesn't see where I am

she's blindfolded

this is what she wants

this is what she needs

and her needs have been met

Express

love me

like a druggy

hug me

like a huggie

snug me

then rub my teletubbie

the heat of your fireplace

is why you are my first place

3:00am

wonder if you will ever

dream away

The sound of the flowers

in bloom
we are doing only what's best
what's best is the idea of
losing it all

Glass curtain

there

I want to be there

where the sunrises

Bring your leaves and I'll bring our branches

close your eyes

do you feel that

it surrounds us

this forest

this energy at our feet

the smell of oak and fresh waters

things are peaceful for a reason

it wasn't by mistake that we ended up here

that is why we are here and not there

as strong as these trees are they carry great roots

how strong your roots are depended and decided

how tall and strong you will be

allow your branches to grow its leaves

and let the wind guide you

green, blue, yellow

another beautiful yellow sunny day
as we enjoy the sun gaze amongst our gold skin
giving us the glow
allowing us to keep shinning
you're there
and I'm here
though I never want to leave from here
never want to leave from this place where I lay
on the green grass looking at the blue and the yellow

Reptile

the lies
you became so comfortable in it
that you started to sleep with it
the lies you used when you told me
that everything was okay
and had nothing to worry about
making me believe in the Disney make believe
happily ever after
drama movies like the Notebook and
Love & Basketball were all real
this isn't sadness
this is rage
the lies
the liess
the liesss

Suffering sadness

oh heartache

how I love/hate you so

allow me to see so many

things at such a small yet

big time depending on the pain

suffering people that we are

we are just suffering in sadness

Summers cry

tears from a woman is so strong
it killed me to hear love cry
there was enough pain in that cry that made me cry
I started to do all I can to make sure I couldn't hear
that painful cry again
just as things were looking so perfect
we started to say our goodbyes to one another

Exchanges

recklessly I fell into the act of love so easily
the want of it when I was at a few years back
became a need of necessity
so surrender yourself to me
endlessly

Change

there's always room for improvement

keep the change

Greater lighter, greater fighter

refusing to believe in the sickness you gave to many

saying that everyone is infected

the ones who aren't are fighting and recovering

this illness must be stopped

it can be stopped if there is some sort of change

My shine

I love rain

those beautiful long showers

that came from a transitioning

of sprinkle and raindrops

it gives great feeling

a great healing

she's all mine

my liquid sunshine

the Red letter

your lips

I love when you dimple

they're so tempting

those lips

they are meant to be kissed by me repeatedly

I want to taste and get hooked

but right now

I just want to feast

this brings to you such great amusement I see

come to me now

here is where you'll come

in this box you will see the outfit I want you to wear

on the box there will be a note reading *take these*

- she smiles

Bring the rain

I'll bring the thunder

just make sure you

bring the noise

The happening

“Let’s just go.” She says to me in such great excitement

“Go? Go where?”

“Does it matter?” She responds. “Let’s take a trip. Do a tour somewhere.

Let’s just get out of here.” That’s when I started to smile to her.

I got up from the couch where we were sitting and walked in the room.

“Girl you crazy! Where would we go? Where would we stay? We aren’t rich you know?

Last time I checked money doesn’t grow on trees.” Looking around the corner of the room I see

Her and I know she is either pouting or mocking me. Either way she’s not satisfied...good.

I came from around the room with my shoes on my feet, wallet in one hand, and keys in the

other. "See! You aren't even ready to go. You're still sitting with that look like you can't believe

this is really happening face."

poetry

a wonderful transition

an epic rhythm combining composition

introduces itself to the beautiful world of poetry

another world where it activates itself

into the world you live in

wishes

kisses are the wishes

we hoped and desire

through the earth, wind, and fire

A night off

whenever we had a hard time seeing the stars at night
we would walk around the city
the beautiful lights on the building were our stars
the weather was cold that night
and the streets were a little wet from the rain
it honestly made the night even more beautiful seeing
the lights reflect off the water
when we kissed it was just that
wet warm and passionate
after the release from the lips you paused
and so did everything else

Houston

thanking God for the wake up in the morning
just to see the night
the lights get bright
and the swift movements on the train makes
buildings show its best for the skylight
everything around the city is so unpredictable
that I can never be miserable
I'm reminded constantly to be someone instead of
being somebody
taking mental notes that I'm not just anybody
I will never get tired of the slangs and swangs near
the dome
I swear there's no place like home

signature signs

no matter how many signs are being put up in our
lives we will always seem to struggle
on where to go
you can tell us that the sign points left but will it ever
feel right
we can let the signs point us to go right but will it be
the right way
signs of go
telling us to not hesitate and debate
signs of slow
telling us to take your time and ease your way
through so you won't miss out
signs of stop telling us to wait and be patient
all signs are important in our lifestyle

we must choose which sign would be the best sign
for the right time

Lost and found

there's so much we can learn from the past
both good and bad
everything has treasure

vibrations

silence is a beautiful thing
to not hear but to feel
feel outside the physical
surrounding yourself spiritual
it reminds me of water
this is wind

Feel

the art of reading words is incredible
its literally described as looking into the clouds
you end up seeing one thing
and it turns into more than what you see
turns out to be more of what you can feel

Blue nature skies

the view is beautiful up here
I can feel the skies as the view fills in the room with
It's cool mysteries
the bathtub sits next to the tall window
The Weeknd plays as the water starts to fill up the tub
while she's in it
gazing out into her world

Trance, thought, vision, illusion

every dream is a lesson
every lesson is a blessing
everything happens for a reason

Love, me

loving everything about you while you are out loving
everyone else
it's time for me to love me

Expectation meets aspiration and optimism

build your faith through your hope
your hope isn't your expectation
more so a belief
expectation leads into a vision of
finding yourself at disappointment
hope gives you vision
it is believing without seeing
eventually you'll create a
greater skill called optimism

Tuesday

today she became her

the girl who you once knew

has become alive more than ever

the great awakening happened

when she opened her eyes and got out of bed

she walked in the bathroom

and saw herself in the mirror

she usually asks herself

who are you every day but this day she says to herself

you are who you are

that's when she knew her life changed

Mortality

life is a dark beautiful light that will eventually dim

it can be a fatal paradise that gives love and death

how you choose to sleep at night depicts on

what happens the next day

don't settle for ordinary

when you have the choice of extraordinary

you make the difference

now go

make a difference

November 11, 2018

Driving sober

Tired and exhausted from the day that lead into the night. It was a beautiful day but more of a beautiful night as I drove us home. Even with the dangerous condition I had a mission and that was for us to get here.

"Oh my God!" you said to me from the backseat. "Turn this up! This is my favorite song by him!" I couldn't help but to laugh at how you sounded. "No seriously this is my song man. It means a lot to me. Would you like to know why?" not out of curiosity I asked him why, but it was something strange that came over me that should ask him why, so he could vent to me. "Great memories come from this song. My best friend before he passed away a few days ago used to jam this song all the time and he would have us listening to this song all the time. Every time we got in the car with him you will more than likely hear this song play at least once or twice." The story hit me a little deeper than I expected and threw me completely left.

I had a mission to get this man home safe. I'm glad I was the person you had a chance to trust to take you home that night. I had a great time singing the song with you. Hope you're doing well out there wherever you are. Until then, take care my friend.

Dear God,

please save a spot for me

I know there aren't many spots left but

I am trying to do my best here

to do everything and anything to be with you

for an eternity

for your glory I will do anything

for your grace I will do everything

the road you gave to me was meant for me

why you choose to bless me with this path is beyond

me

but I thank you

thank you for all you've done for me

for the life of the now and for the life of hereafter

Guardians

you're my teacher

my listener

the observer who graduated and became my professor

all through my childhood you were my guardians

many places I could be

but I know where I am and where I will be

thank you

for all you've done for me

Random Challenges

I overcame my fears and made it to the new levels
what they keep forgetting to mention
is the new devils
I met one and she was beautiful
she wore a lighter skin
but still resembled the melanin like me
it was a fall season that was falling
closer to the winter
these seasons are deadly for me
though I didn't care
I knew what I was getting myself into
what I fell into and what I fell into was her

she was my new level

my devil

Sooner than later

close your eyes
and let the stillness surround you
let your breathing be found and heard
acknowledge the fact that you have grown
you aren't where you use to be
I'm proud of you
you'll get there
sooner than later

Day

a beautiful day

I can see her everyday

each day, day by day

Look up

no matter what happens

5am

good morning early blue birds

you are here for a reason

whatever it is make it last each season

Vision

I see the white sky

I can feel the wind blowing

it is snowing

December 01

the older you get you realize the job that you worked
or may currently be working in is worth something
I can't say it was meant for nothing because nothing
is still something
how you live your life though within the next few
months in labor defines your skills
define your definition of grind
refuse to be like the rest of the world trapped in the
mind

Food

how you feed yourself spiritually determines your health

Ticktock

we don't have time to waste
to go after something or someone that isn't worth the chase
timing is everything

Teach, learn, burn

your education brought us deflation and segregation
depression with no lesson
what have you taught us within the years
that if we pass the class we are suddenly ready
ready for what
the world
which world
the dreamworld or the underworld

The garden

welcome to the garden of Eden

the garden of peace and beauty

that creates love

a love within this garden

we will grow and plant our seeds

watching our flowers grow with strong roots

let's create this beautiful life together

Snow

she enjoys the snow

to be honest we both do

the things it does to people of the winter

brings out the best

holidays became the best days

now they're just a memory

that became my worst days

Mr. Freeze

the pain you give to me I've became so numb to it

I've become so cold

Future galaxies

let me take you to a familiar
place out of space
show me your galaxy
and I'll show you my stars

Dedication/motivation

I can become your dedication

your motivation

keep your eyes on me and

I'll get you there

from there to here

Ascent

referring my goals as mountains for a reason
I vision the path we must take just to get there
I can see it from a distance
but I know that I must go
through some sort of valley
some sort of great travel
that may have myself wondering if it's all worth it
then I'll remember those who made it to the peak
with the troubles and climbs
they too had to go through before they reached their goal

War

every day is a fight

you're either fighting yourself

to overcome your fears and

reach your goals or you're

training yourself to accept the lies you keep telling

yourself that It's too hard or its impossible

this is a battle

this is a fight that you must put up with yourself

you are the enemy of your own opponent

the man in the mirror

train yourself mentally so you will know how to react

physically

spiritually you must be awake

take the time to know yourself

this is how you grow yourself

Heroism

without the vision

one simply wouldn't know where to go

Inside

courage to grow or to run and go

February 04, 2019

she’s not meant for everybody

but she is meant for somebody

Wine glass

her lips touched the glass

with a taste

she touches and taste her glass

I am her wine glass

Read, Red

sit your bag down

take your watch and bracelets off

your earrings and your necklace off

your heels on the other hand may stay on

when I come back there will be no dress

yes

"yes"

One

I want you to see my growth

I want you to feel my growth

feel my growth

see my growth

Star shine

we look forward to the weekends of night wonders
never actually understanding the trends
and how things work with the people we encounter
however
this isn't the case
while we are out into the night we listen
to the movement of water and how it flows silently
hitting the shore
you never get a chance to understand how beautiful
things can be
until it starts to shine in the night

Soular

her ordinary became my extraordinary
whenever she danced
she singed
whenever she singed
she danced
there may have been that one guy who saw her
but he didn’t see her worth
a love that defines the sea
a solar of energy

Lovers fantasy

let's get out of this place and
let's go out of space
let's use this spaceship
and travel the universe and get shipwrecked
let's get lost in our reality
our fantasy

Universal Unconditional

I traveled through such great distance to reach your
greatness and I've heard stories about your travel
how you overcame your troubles and struggles
how you fought with a cause and a purpose
you understood everything and made it become
natural
nothing was by accident and everything serves a
purpose
with this purpose we overcame the natural
and became welcomed in the supernatural

Good morning

the sunrise will rise

in your eyes I began to rise

the sun feels brighter than a Sunday

I slept next to you

now I am waking up to you

this is a good morning

Wanna get to be crazy in love

I want to get to know you

steal your love

drive you crazy

crazy in love

Letter L

show me another world

show me to your place

I want to make your universe swirl

Lights and waves

listen

listen closely

listen closely to the stillness in the room

feel

feel the movement

feel the movement that surrounds you

combine the two and receive the light waves

Nature and creation

I got a taste of what your mind is like and I liked it
it made me want to dive deep into your soul
your spirit was highly lifted once it was matched
you even showed me how sweet your energy is
your body is well crafted and perfectly fit
I want it

seem

watching last night sky stars were phenomenal

watching you glow from the sunrises touch is

unforgettable

Novelty and royalty

you've became one of the best books I've ever read

May

may the love come to you and may it never get lost

from you

She

my heart is a she

and she is the reason

why I am alive today

Creator of nature

by looking at her I then saw the power of God

B.P

I love being black and beautiful

March 11, 2019

self-care is the best care

a happy life is a healthy life

you

no matter who you are

no matter where you are

I hope when you read this poem it brings you

peace

love

and prosperity

June 15, 2019

I am alive

less than but Greater Than

I am my greatest enemy

The Good, The Badd, The Ugly, The Worst

I'm scared

a little scarred but I'm mostly scared

what if they treat me like that

what if I'm on to something and I get caught

they tell me to do all these things that I don't want to

do

my vision is clear but I want it to be cloudy and be

like the majority of the rich

born to be better is why I'm wealthy

I've been damaged but I'm still living healthy

this is a message

a letter for anyone who feels like they are alone

for anyone who feels like they have whatever light
they have left in them
we are who we are and we will make the best of it
we must get them to make the best
out of themselves
remember to breathe
breathe slowly and deeply
you will make it
I believe in you

June 11, 2019

the waves were picking up from the cool wind

I sat and watched it thinking I could be part of it all

the cool wind

the waves

the sky

I wanted to be part of it

that's when I started to feel it all

that is when I became it all

Levels of 50

legendary of legacy this is the start of a legendary

legacy

here is one

two

you’re lonely

I’ve become aware of that

to overcome the lonely nights

the late nights

the ponder

that makes you wonder

lost in the Alice

lost in space

universe of this verse

poetry lives

Count three

another life

this is the life I chose

the one I've become and grown

I flown into another place that seems lost

eventually becoming the found

cheers

four

truth is this is the truth

accept what you want out of it and allow it to be what

is meant to be

what you desire is on the other side of the fire

the flame is big but so is your heart

drive through your fears

get through the rain

this is your world

you are the creator of your pain

count five

awake my love

awaken my love

awaken the love

awake our love

six

breathe in love and never exhale it

never let go of the love because of the hate

count seven

at times I find myself in a dark place
never do I attend to stay there either
I’ve seen it hurt many people because they have
convinced and convince themselves its safer
they believe since they are in a hurt place
they are in a safe place

eight

take the time out to make time for yourself

all great things take time

Count nine

heal yourself

the pain is temporary

it won't last forever

ten

to do what you want is out of the ordinary

it's completely an extraordinary

count eleven

he may not tell you this

just as she may not tell you this either but

you are worth it

you deserve it

twelve

the sun needs its rest too

rest light

count thirteen

I don’t want to run from it anymore

running only makes things worse

fourteen

who I am is who I decide to become

I've got the universe on my side

I've got God on the inside

Count fifteen

the hate that is brought to the light is less not lesser

sixteen

dear self

love

Count seventeen

follow me on the words to the journey of your
greatness
I am on the path of righteousness for thy name sake
as it is said that the creator will never leave me nor
forsake

eighteen

I've seen man become so strong that he decides to take a knee for the one he loves

Count nineteen

I've also witnessed man take a knee for the people he loves

twenty

respect those who have come before you

no one is beneath you

if so

you are beneath someone

Count twenty-one

accept who you are

for you are one

twenty-two

in the face of the clouds

I felt wind that was able to help me breathe

in the horizon the visual of creation shined at its best

unforgettable timing

unforgettable moment

Count twenty-three

don’t wait for me if you aren’t going to be there

twenty-four

in your eyes I saw the yellow

your favorite color

it was alive and vibrant

then I saw the coldness take over

everything seemed so dead inside

Count twenty-five

she was someone I knew and became someone new
hopefully things will become natural
in her natural state of mind

twenty-six

in the count of days that we departed
I've started to make things clear
even though she was willing to stay
she was lost in the ways of her past
the life she lived was different than other girls
she became addicted to the things
that were temporary
she was aware of her surroundings
but just like a drug she had to have more of it
I couldn't blame her

Count twenty-seven

this became the time of the unforgettable moment
the forgettable but never unforgivable

Admitting (twenty-eight)

the past has a funny way of showing itself into the
most present of times
at this time I've become a little cooler in the sun
not the brightest of light forms
but still able to gain and maintain
to give and receive
the past brought itself into the present of the image of
the unforgettable when I met a light
it was because of my past I ended up making that
light not so bright
these are some of the things that man can't talk about
this is something I've become to do to help myself
out

Count twenty-nine

the pain I've caused I know I won't be able to undo
I hate what I have done to you
what I've done to us
you forgive and it seems so hard to believe when I
have a hard time forgiving myself

thirty

you lost me when you said goodbye

Count thirty-one

in the dark tunnel there is a light at then end

there are obstacles you must face before reaching the

end of that tunnel

thirty-two

believe it or not monsters are real
hiding them and acting like they don't exist won't
help because they are everywhere
when you admit that they are real it may become
easier through your understanding
these are the reasons why you stay up at night
these are the reasons why you leave your light on at
night

Count thirty-three

she remains hidden inside of her shell because she
knows that this is what they want
this is what he wants

thirty-four

giving up isn't an option for me anymore

it was some time ago

although I've got out of that dark tunnel

still I remember the hell

and what I must do to get out

I am happy that I am out of there

and I will never go back there

that is why giving up isn't an option for me anymore

Count thirty-five

the sun started to shine a little different and my skin
brought out a beautiful glow to my body
surrounding itself to me with its magnetic energy
allowing me to feel certain waves with someone
the energy was kinetic and we connected
I'm starting to feel myself love again
but like the other ones I had before her I halt
I wasn't sure where we were going
the worst part about it was that I was loving it
I love to love but I am not a fan of loving what isn't
loving me back

thirty-six

but just like my past I gave in

Count thirty-seven

regrets exist

I felt like I wasn't supposed to say that but it does in

the mind at certain times

because I was living a certain way

didn't plan to be selfish

didn't want to be foolish

thirty-eight

here I am now

and there I was loving her

loving and loving her

Count thirty-nine

I’ve practically drove myself insane for the love of
her game
a certain light that I couldn’t get enough of
even though she felt so little towards me
I made her know that she was my little one

forty

she told me how trash the men and women were
before me
what they would say and do to her to make her
become so low
that's when it hit me that it wasn't me being
dominant and making her little
it was the people she was with that made her feel so
low inside
here comes the rain

Count forty-one

a love fool I was not knowing where I was heading
but I knew I wasn’t heading into the wrong directions
with the decisions I was making
different from most men I became the man that other
men wanted to be like
yet I still wasn’t the man I wanted to be like
and she became more of the woman I wanted my
daughter to be like
she was the mother that made me think I was father
to a son

forty-two

I was there with her through it all
the clash with her jobs and family seemed like they
weren't ever going away from her
but when she talked to me through the day it seemed
like her problems went away

Count forty-three

opening to someone is the worst for some reason
at least from this prospective
I've became attached to someone who was attached
to me
letting out all the old and bringing in the new
this was new to me
I mean I've done this before
It was just different since it hasn't been done with her
but I am ready for the things to come and I've learned
how to fight the demons that were
attaching themselves to me
I'm ready for the future
hopefully she is too

A life to live (More to live a life)

there is never truly an ending to anything nor is there really an ending of anyone. anything and everyone exist with a purpose that leads itself towards another appearance of existence. it took me some time to find out why I even existed. now that I am aware of my existence and why I appear here to the world I want to say thank you. thank you to those I have met and have encountered. In some form of way I have learned a lot in such small time. there is still so much to learn from this existence of which I exist. as long as I may continue amongst this life I promise to provide a life and save a life.

V

Also made by s.v.h

In The Venting

Book I

www.ingramcontent.com/pod-product-compliance
Lightning Source LLC
Chambersburg PA
CBHW032004050726
47590CB00006B/2042

* 9 7 8 1 7 3 5 0 1 9 8 1 9 *